"WE HAVE SO MUCH FUN WITH MY DAD THAT I WISHT I HAD KNOWN HIM SOONER. He is a farmer. He smells like a cow, and when I smell that cow in the house, I know Pop is home and I am glad.

"My pop's tops because every time I ast for a knickel he will start preeching that when he was a boy he had to earn his knickels, and at the same time he is putting his hand in his pocket and pulls out a knickel for me.

"My pop's tops because he was a brave soldier. He didn't see me till I was three years old, yet he is just as good to me as if he knew me all my life."

A Dad is for Spending Time With

DR. CHARLIE SHEDD

ace books

A Division of Charter Communications Inc
A GROSSET & DUNLAP COMPANY
51 Madison Avenue
New York, New York 10010

CONTENTS

Preface

"What is a dad for?" That was the question.

I am a minister and in this capacity I can ask questions. I have a chance to talk with the young, including little people. This particular Sunday School class was a junior group. Very alert. Since I was their pastor and friend, their vibrations were good.

Answers:

"A dad is for telling you 'not to' when you don't pay attention to your mother after she has already said you shouldn't." "A dad is for going to work so everybody can eat and wear clothes and sometimes he will buy you something." "A dad is for sitting with your mother and discussing things which they do not want you to hear."

Twenty children with twenty plus ideas. And since that hour I've asked it again with fascinating results. But one of my favorites is:

"A DAD IS FOR SPENDING TIME WITH."

This book reports on fathers from all over the United States and Canada. These stories come from children, high schoolers, the college set, wives, and sometimes fathers themselves, writing to my newspaper column "Strictly for Dads."

If you could read my mail, I am sure you would feel as I do. Hopeful. Excited. You would thrill that so many men these days want to be good fathers.

CHARLIE W. SHEDD
Skidaway Island, Georgia
1978

CHAPTER 1

Ten Traits of One Neat Dad

More than anything else what would a child appreciate about his father?

Interesting question with some fascinating answers. Our *One Neat Dad* contest brings hundreds of letters from children and teenagers.

After twelve months I'm beginning to hear certain steady refrains. Themes repeating themselves. As a father myself I need all the help I can get. So here's a list of the ten most appreciated qualities for "one neat dad."

1. He takes time for me
2. He listens to me
3. He plays with me
4. He invites me to go places with him
5. He lets me help him
6. He treats my mother well
7. He lets me say what I think
8. He's nice to my friends

9. He only punishes me when I deserve it

10. He isn't afraid to admit it when he's wrong

Note: Qualities one to five are versions of the single word, *Time*!

These dads are hard workers. They're on the go, earning a living, serving their community, doing church work. Plus they're men with hobbies. They golf. They fish, hunt, work with wood. But, though they are busy and into an infinite variety of extras, these are dads who take time for their children.

Quotes direct from where it's happening:

"When my father has something to do, he will ask me to help him. He will say, 'Come and hold these boards for me' or 'Let's wash the car.' So I help him and lots of times he even helps me when I have something to do such as homework or chores."

"My dad is a rancher and he has a lot to do. But I really like it when he says, 'Jump in the pickup, Betsy. I've got to go to town for some parts.' I think that is neat, because some of my friends' fathers never invite them to go anywhere."

"The thing I like best about my dad is that he will always let me talk to him. My friends think this is so great, they will even come and talk with him too. That helps a lot, because you understand things better when you have someone to tell them to."

Spell it "listen," spell it "play," spell it "help me," spell it "jump in the pickup." It all comes out with the same four letters—*Time*. And it is *the* single most appreciated trait of One Neat Dad.

CHAPTER 2

Will You Read to Me?

"Daddy, will you read to me?" Every little girl is sure to ask it one day. And isn't this amazing? She always asks it when we're busy.

I remember an incident with Karen when she was four.

There was an important meeting and I had promised the committee chairman I would meet him early. As I put my hand on the knob, she turned on all her charm. "Daddy," she said, "will you read to me?" The usual excuses formed on my lips, but what came out was, "Sure, honey, I'll read to you."

So I read. Short book, five chapters, and it couldn't have taken more than three minutes to go through chapter one. Then I closed the book and said, "Gee, that's an exciting story. I can hardly wait to see how it comes out. Do you think you can wait?" "Oh," she answered, "I already know how it comes out. Mommy reads me that one all the time."

How blind can a daddy be? She didn't want to know

what the book said. The information she wanted was something else. Did she matter more than a dumb old meeting?

Sure, fathers have some things which must be done by deadline. But the question is: What is more important than a little girl? To which there is only one answer—Nothing! *

So how can we give the time for effective fathering? Well, here's one answer—*it won't get done without scheduling*!

Would you be willing to experiment with this for a fair try? One date per month with each of your children.

Dinner out alone. Lunch. Breakfast. Then to a show, a game, the store for some shopping. Anywhere they want to go.

This could be one of the finest father decisions you ever made. And if you begin at two, that will make almost two hundred times by the time your children finish high school.

In two hundred visits you can become "best friends."

* Story adapted from Dr. Shedd's book, *You Can Be A Great Parent* (Word, Inc., 1970).

CHAPTER 3

Interruptions

"Daddy, will you read to me?"

"I need help with my homework."

"Can you take me to the store for a tablet?"

"Come fix my bicycle."

"How about a game of checkers?"

These we have always with us. Askings, demands, appeals, petitions, requests. By any name they are very much a part of fathering.

How we react to these continual interruptions may depend on some basic prethink. So here are two questions for shaping our philosophy:

1. *If our children never interrupted, we wouldn't really like that either, would we?*

I know two dads whose time is never broken in on now. One has built up such a wall between himself and his children, they wouldn't think of bothering him. In that home, every request, every little problem, is channeled through the mother.

The other dad lost his child two years ago, his only child. That dad would give everything he has for one interruption.

2. *Most of the time (like ninety-five percent) aren't the interrupter and his interruption more important than what we're doing?*

Sure, there are days when we're into something crucial. Some things do have to be done pronto! But even then, we can give a positive answer; take a minute to explain; set a time when we can get to it.

Most of us would like to be among those serene people going through life easy-like, welcoming all who need us. And we would also like our children to have about them an aura of quiet balance, inner peace, openness.

Maybe this would be a very good day for a family discussion on:

Are we, all of us, interruptible enough around here?

CHAPTER 4

Togetherness at the First Heartbeat

Today's winner in our "One Neat Dad" contest isn't a father yet. But he's going to be. And here's the report from Charleston, S.C.

"Dear Dr. Shedd:

"For the past few months I've been enjoying, smiling, and sometimes crying over all the nominees for your One Neat Dad contest. One thing strikes me as being totally left out of the winner columns I've read and I think it's a basic question: When does a man become a father?

"I'd like to nominate my husband for One Neat Dad even though we haven't met our child yet, because he/she hasn't arrived in the regular sense. I'm not due to deliver for another three months, but David is so interested in everything. My friends say they have never seen anything like it.

"I still work and David does so much to make life easier for me. He helps with dinner, the dishes, the housework.

17

He goes with me to the expectant parent classes, helps me with the exercises they teach us, and we study the books together.

"He even keeps the doctor's appointments with me. And here's one thing I think is so nice. We heard our child's heartbeat together the first time in the doctor's office. That's a moment I'll never forget and I am sure he won't either.

"Well, I thought since your column reaches so many fathers I should write you about David. Maybe in your vast circle of readers there would be other fathers who would like to give some serious thought to prenatal love and care from their side.

"Do you know what I wonder sometimes? I wonder if the baby knows already that we both care so much. It gives me such a secure feeling to think about the kind of father our child will have. Plus I can tell you that living with a man like this is true happiness when you're pregnant or otherwise."

CHAPTER 5

Family Night at the Svendsens

Every week with no exception the Svendsens have "Family Night." On Sunday they decide when it will be, and the whole gang has agreed to this ritual.

Because I know the Svendsens well, I decided to do an interview. I asked each member of the family for their personal reactions to "Family Night."

Paul, Junior: "Sometimes when my friends want me to go out, I just tell them I can't go. This is 'Family Night.' You would think they might think that is strange, but they never say anything, and I will tell you why. It is because most of them don't have a very close family, and they would like to be the way we are. I will also tell you something else. I believe it gives you confidence when you really belong to a group like our family. You feel good because they understand you.

"My father travels a lot. Sometimes when he is going to be gone, we will have Family Night on Sunday and then he waits till Monday to leave. Sometimes we have it on Friday, so he can get back home to be with us.

"During football season our whole family comes to the games, and my dad hasn't missed one time since I was in high school. I think that is really great. Every single time I played he was there."

Cindy (a high school sophomore): "You want to know why I like Family Night? Well, it is because you get very close to each other when you spend so much time together. You see, I don't do a lot of things like my brother Paul. He is on the football team and stuff like that. Barbara Ann plays cymbals in the band. What I like to do is study and listen to records and talk on the phone. I also play tennis, but I do not go out for the team, and I don't want to. I think my family is really neat because even if we are all different, that's O.K. When you know each other, you don't worry that everybody should be alike.

"A lot of my friends don't like their mother. Well, I don't feel that way because most of the time even she and I can talk. I feel like I understand her, and she understands me better."

Barbara Ann (age twelve): "I like Family Night because when you don't like something, you can wait till that night and tell everyone. Then you discuss it and vote. That is really great, because usually they will understand what you are saying. Sometimes they don't vote for you, but when you listen to them, you can see why it maybe wasn't such a good idea anyway. I also like Family Night, because our whole family comes to the band concert. Then we go out afterward and have a good time."

Craig (age nine): "The thing I like is that we have so

much fun together, even my mom and dad."

Then this final word, flashing back to Barbara Ann:

"We really do like each other better. I even like Craig sometimes."

CHAPTER 6

Gathering in the Parents' Bedroom

Margo and Phil have five children. And do they ever have fun! Hobbies, games, songs, trips, plus a miscellany of family-invented rituals.

But maybe the biggest ritual is their weekly party in the parents' bedroom. Every Saturday morning, early. Coffee for mom and dad, hot chocolate for the children. Visiting, laughing, planning, and just plain being together.

Margo and Phil love children, so they adopted two and the oldest of their tribe is six. When I heard their story, I asked where this Saturday morning thing originated and here's what Margo told me:

"The number one memory of my childhood is our weekly get-togethers in my parents' bedroom, and lest you think it was only when we were little, I guess I ought to tell you we did it clear up through high school. Even when we came home from college, we did it.

"Plus, I'll never forget the first time Phil was in on one of these events. We were engaged and I'd taken him home for a weekend. He said, 'Margo, I've never seen anything like it. We've got to be sure when we have our family, we'll never be too busy for things like that.'

"So," says Margo, "that's why we gather every Saturday in our bedroom, Phil and I, and the children, the dog, and a cat or two. Sometimes on Sunday we do it too.

"Phil is crazy about golf and fishing and sports of every kind. He also likes to work in his shop. But he won't let anything interfere with our Saturday morning ritual."

There are fathers whose family history has a negative effect on their own fathering. They say, "We never did it when I was a kid, so why should we now?"

But then there are other dads who, looking back, reason: "I want the best for my children. Let's do it a better way."

CHAPTER 7

Treasure Hunts

Holidays can be great times for the family. Christmas, Easter, Fourth of July, Thanksgiving. Plus anniversaries, birthdays, special occasions.

But those who remember their homes with a glow will probably tell us something else. They'll take us back to the *little* celebrations, regular get-togethers, *small* items which meant so much as they were growing up.

One way to create stable children is to provide happy memories. Since that is true, then "fun" can be one all-important word for the best kind of parenting.

Today's column is about "treasure hunts." If you have small children, you might build up some wonderful long-term recall with "treasure hunts."

Procedure:

Dad stops on way home to buy big sack of penny candies, balloons, bubble gum, peanuts, plus other minor items children go for. One of every kind for each child.

When dinner is over, troops make for bedroom while mom and dad hide treasure. Under chairs, behind lamps, on window sills, mostly in plain sight, but some well hidden.

Each child is given a sack, and youngest has head start as dad counts to ten. Competition is keen for who finds the most, but no prize because after the hunt is over everyone pours loot on sheet in middle of floor. Then they take turns dividing evenly.

For parents with grown children it's interesting to note where the conversation leads at family get-togethers. Is it the big things? The colossal? The high celebrations?

Usually not.

Next time you're with a family whose children are out of the home and are back now for a visit, listen to what they're saying. Check it out. Isn't it amazing how much of their talk centers in simple little memories? And often they are memories of plain, ordinary, home-made fun!

CHAPTER 8

Preplanning Time Together

Wohlford is a traveling executive. He's an island hopper in the purest sense. He does his thing in the Caribbean. The Bahamas, Bimini, Antigua, Haiti, Guadalupe, Grand Cayman, St. Vincent's. His headquarters are in Jamaica, where he lives with his two boys, two girls, and a wife who says, "I nominate Wohlford for One Neat Dad. We all think he is just great."

It always gives me a special thrill when I hear some woman say that about her husband. But this one comes out of such an unusual setting, it's worth another look.

Almost every week Wohlford goes somewhere. Occasionally because of distance, he's gone two weeks in a row. Yet his family keeps on saying, "He's the greatest."

How does he do it? Last time I heard them bragging on this ususual dad, I decided to get it straight from where it's happening.

This is Wohlford's report:

"With us it's a matter of planning. Several times each

year we have a conference when we schedule our time together. Weekends, whole weeks, trips, special events. Almost every week I get calls to come to somebody's rescue. But do you know how I handle this kind of short notice? I tell people, 'This is family week and I can't come.' It's amazing how they can make do when they have to.

"Of course, there are some emergencies and I must go. So if it will interrupt prearranged family time, we work a trade or reschedule to make up for my absence. I think the main thing with the family is to let them know you care, that even when you have to be gone, you would prefer to be with them. If they know you mean it, they will understand, make adjustments, and all of this doesn't widen the gaps between you. It brings you closer together."

We have had reports from men who set up calendars with their families monthly, weekly, even daily. But for some of us Wohlford's long-range planning may be just the thing for a better kind of long-range fathering.

CHAPTER 9

Training in Democracy

Straight from the teen scene—two letters. My correspondence comes from fathers, mothers, grandpas, grandmas, plus some exciting mail from the young set.

Here are two from opposite ends of the discipline spectrum. This girl is wondering where the boundaries are:

"Dear Dr. Shedd:

"Do you think it's possible for a girl to be unhappy because she can do anything she wants? My parents never ground me like my friends get grounded. They never say 'no' about anything. Most of my friends think I'm lucky. But sometimes it scares me to be able to go anywhere and do everything with no one telling me when to stop."

Now here's a boy weary with dictatorship:

"Dear Dr. Shedd:

"Do you know how terrible it is to live with a father

who is always right? My dad thinks he is like Jesus Christ, but I think he is more like Hitler. All of us kids hate him. And do you know what I think? I think my mom does too. It seems like a lot of my friends have the same problem and a lot of them are on drugs. Sometimes I don't blame them. Believe me, next year when I go away to college, I'm going to let it all hang out."

Where's the fine line? How much authority do our kids need? Maybe the need is different in different homes. But right now I'd like to ring the bells for some good old-fashioned American democracy in our fathering.

Would you be willing to try this as an experiment?

Announce to the tribe that for ninety days you're going to do something new. The whole family will decide what's fair, what's good, what's right. Every person will have one vote. Voting will be by ballot, anonymous. Anyone can bring up anything anytime.

Sounds scary?

It is. But as your experiment proceeds, I think you'll agree these sons and daughters we're raising have a rare sense of wisdom when we give it a chance to surface. In questions relating to the good of everyone, they make very few mistakes. On decisions relating to themselves they are much more likely to accept the family vote than an edict from dad and mom. Dictatorship is much faster than democracy and less frightening if you're the dictator.

But for any dad with the courage to do it, this ninety-day trial could be worth some serious thought. It might even develop into an exciting new life style for everyone in the family.

CHAPTER 10

Papa Loves Us All and Each One of Us Alone

This story is written by Tammy. She's seventeen.
"Dear Dr. Shedd:

"The thing I like about my papa is that he is papa to all our family. But he is also papa to each one of us six girls by ourselves.

"Jacquelyn is the baby, and papa loves her dearly. You should see them walking together at night when he gets home from work. And he also swings her in the backyard all alone.

"Elena is next. She is six. She likes to help papa work on his car. And although she messes up a lot of things, you would think she was the very best kind of helper the way he talks about her. In summer they go to the beach together and he is teaching her how to swim. She'll never be the Olympic champion, but papa doesn't care, and neither does Elena, because they have so much fun together.

"Carmela was the biggest klutz one year ago. Then she said she wanted to play basketball. So papa told her 'I will teach you.' Do you know what he did? He taught her so much that in the last game she scored half the points. We were all there cheering for her. And Carmela said, 'Thank you, papa. No one can ever take this night away from me.'

"The twins are Roxanne and Rosemary. They are fifteen. He does a lot with them together. But that is not all. He also says to them. 'Someday you will marry and you will not be together, so I will show you how to have a good time when you are away from each other.' Then he shows them.

"At last there is me. I am Tammy. I have some strange feelings because I am seventeen. Do you know how it is to be seventeen? Yet I cannot remember one time when papa put me down. He will say, 'I do not think that is a wise thing to do, but I will love you even if you do it.' This makes me think, and do you know what? It even makes me want to do what I know papa thinks is wise.

"Like I said we also do a lot of things together such as going to mass, having picnics, and talk a lot. I guess Italian families like ours enjoy these things especially.

"I also want you to know—as for mama, she loves my papa very much. They spend time together without us, like they will go out on what they call a date, and we can't go. But we do not mind. In fact, usually we like this very much, because if you could see papa and mama together, you would feel good too."

CHAPTER 11

Real Estate Training at Eleven and Nine

Scott is eleven, Becky nine, and they are both know-ledgeable about real estate. For children their age they know an amazing amount first-hand.

Their dad is one of the rising young executives with a paint company. Recently they transferred him again which is the fifth time in thirteen years.

This time it's Detroit. But when it came to house-hunting, Louise couldn't go. She's the children's mother, pregnant, and her doctor didn't want her to make the trip.

So Dave, Scott, and Becky went in search of their new home. Here's Dave's report:

"You'd be surprised at all the things kids notice going through a house, and the questions they ask the real estate agent—they're something else.

"I took them with me to the bank to work out the loan, and to the lawyer. Everyone was really great with the kids. They seemed to get a kick out of it, explained all they wanted to know about mortgages, interest, principal, title insurance, taxes, appraisal. The real estate agent even took us to lunch. I think that impressed them more than anything.

"Maybe I should add they missed three days of classes to get this in. But I'll bet there aren't two other kids in their school know as much about buying a house as Scott and Becky now. That's education too isn't it?"

Sure is. And thanks, Dave, for writing. But thanks even more for giving us a nudge. The price of two tickets to Detroit may be an impossibility for some. But your point comes through loud and clear: The smart dad seizes every opportunity to train his children. And to be with them!

CHAPTER 12

Tax Expert at Thirteen

"You should be teaching in our seminar." That's what the tax man said, and behind his statement is an unusual story.

Robert is a seventh grader. He came home one night and said, "Dad, I wish you would tell me something. I was over at Terry's house and his father came home real mad. Something about an audit and I mean he was really mad. Why would he be like that?"

So here comes an interesting report straight from Robert's dad:

"All of a sudden I realized it must be confusing to a kid when he hears all these things about taxes and doesn't understand any part of it. Right then I decided to make a project of teaching Robert what I could. After all, as long as he lives he's going to need to know about taxes, tax laws, tax forms, paying taxes.

"So we had several sessions and I told him all I knew.

Then we went to see a tax expert. He filled in what I left out, answered questions and gave us some material. He also recommended we visit the IRS office. Well we did, and I was surprised. First because they would take so much time with us, but more than that because Robert knew enough to ask some very intelligent questions.

"This term at school he wrote a paper on taxes. It was so good that when I showed our tax expert friend, he told Robert, 'You ought to be teaching in our seminars. Why don't you think about a career in taxes?'

"Of course, this got Robert excited. I know I'm bragging, but I think I have a right to be proud of the way he went after this tax business."

I think you have a right to be proud of him too.

And proud of yourself.

Taking the time to move in on a child's questions like this dad did has to be extra good fathering.

CHAPTER 13

Jimmy, the Woodcutter

Straight out of the woods, a winner.

Jimmy is thirteen and he is into an unusual project. It's been a hard winter and this young entrepreneur has capitalized on the cold. With the help of his father, he has launched a healthy business in firewood.

How they got onto this was one casual comment of a friend. The man was clearing a home site, getting ready to fell some trees, and in a hurry. So Jimmy and his dad offered to do the job—"We keep the wood." From there Jimmy took over. He bought a used chain saw (the safest kind possible), and when the word got out, he could hardly keep up with orders. After school. Saturdays. Vacations.

Tell us about it, Jimmy—

"Well, it is a good business and kind of fun, but not all of it. Like you can't always goof off with your friends and you never get to sleep on Saturday morning. But I have learned a lot. I have learned about saws and how to keep them sharp. And I have learned you should be very careful with them. Now, I'm thinking about buying a new saw so I am looking at different kinds.

"When I started, I did not know what a 'rack' of wood was, or a 'cord.' But now I know. My father taught me how to stack wood so the water will run off and the air can get to it.

"I have also learned a lot about running a business. I mean such as putting an ad in the paper and taking orders on the phone, and saving money. Probably what you learn most is all the different kinds of people there are, and how to talk with them and keep them thinking you are O.K. to do business with.

"There is something else about this I like and it is that my dad lets me do it all myself except he drives the pickup when we haul the wood and make deliveries. That gives us a chance to visit and he tells me a lot of things. I like that too."

CHAPTER 14

Doctor of the Left Ear

Ever hear of a doctor of the left ear? I have.

I was giving an after-dinner speech and the soloist turned me on with his beautiful tenor voice. This guy could really sing.

They introduced him as a physician. So when the evening was over, I told him how much I appreciated his singing. Then I asked, "What kind of doctor are you?" Grinning, he answered, "I am a doctor of the left ear."

"Come again," I said, "You're putting me on!"

"Well, sort of," he agreed. "But I am an eye, ear, nose, and throat specialist. My partner and I have a deal. When a new patient comes in, if it's his right ear, he goes to my partner. Left ear, I get him. That's why I call myself 'Doctor of the Left Ear.' "

Far out, but this is a day of specialization and experts tell us that tomorrow's world will be even more so.

What's the message for dads? Maybe a good one.

I'm with the college set frequently, and it surprises me sometimes how many of this group have no idea what field they want to go into.

So what can a dad do about this vacuum?

I know an electrical engineer who was recently named president of his company and he gives his father all the credit. Nothing so unusual about that, except in this case, the father never finished high school. What he did do was to get right on with his boy's interest in electricity. When he discovered a natural tendency in this direction, he encouraged it all the way. He taught his son how to splice a cord, wire a lamp, fix plugs.

Then he took him to an electrical plant, introduced him to some experts, went to the library and took out books on the subject.

My electrical engineer friend says, "I have studied under some of the sharpest people in my field. For more than five years I hit the books, and summers I was lucky to get jobs related to what I was studying. But there is no way I can tell you how much I appreciate that early input from my dad.

"I have one son who is interested in animals and another all philosopher. You can bet I am doing everything I can to do for them what my dad did for me. I honestly believe the best career training can start at home."

CHAPTER 15

Alfreda, the Veterinarian

Alfreda graduated from vet school in June. Nothing so unusual about a lady veterinarian. There were three other girls in her class. But here's why I thought Alfreda might have a message strictly for dads:

"It took me eight years to finish, because I had to drop out three times in order to work. That is because I have seven brothers and sisters. I have always loved animals and when I started talking about veterinary medicine way back there, it was almost unheard of for a girl to even think of that. In fact, most of my friends either made fun of me or said it was impossible.

"But not my father. We live on a river and he would take me fishing and say, 'Alfreda don't you let anybody tell you what you can't do. If you study hard enough, work hard enough, and pray hard enough, you can be almost anything you want to be.'

"Then he would help me and we would raise chickens

and ducks and rabbits and pigs. Also we raised coon hounds which we trained and sold. I even had a calf and a few bees.

"If you could know my father, you would realize how hard he worked to help me. He is custodian of our grade school and he preaches in a little country church on Sundays. But he always kept saying, 'Alfreda, you can do it.'

"The day I graduated my mother wasn't able to come, because she has not been well this year. But my father was there, and I know there was not a prouder father anywhere. I can tell you, also, there wasn't a prouder graduate either.

"No matter how long I live, I will always hear my father's words, 'You can do it, Alfreda.' Without those words from him, I would have given up many times."

CHAPTER 16

They Clean the High Windows

The Kubiaks clean windows. It's big business with them and they are way up there. John Kubiak and his four sons work only on skyscrapers. They have all the business they can handle and they make an excellent living.

Three of the four boys are college graduates. Each boy began his training when he reached junior high age. At first, regulations kept him close to ground level. But as soon as he was legally old enough, he began working up, and they all say they wouldn't be doing anything else.

Mark: "Financially, I am doing better than all of my friends, even those who went for their Ph.D.'s. I know money isn't the most important thing in the world, but it sure gives you a good feeling to know you're into a trade nobody can take away from you."

Paul: "You ask if it's boring? Never. Up there we meet more people than you would think, and besides that, it's fascinating to watch what's going on so far below us."

Walter: "I worked as a research chemist for three years after I graduated, but all the time I kept thinking how our family gets along and how we all work together so well.

"Do you know why we get along? From the time each of us started, our father sat us down and told us we could only work for him if we were friends and we felt good about each other. He didn't say we have to agree but he encouraged us to get all our negative feelings out in discussion around our table. From hearing other people talk, I don't believe there's any family that gets along as well as we do. And that's one of the main reasons I decided to come back and stay with it."

Here's a good question for any dad: Am I teaching my family to disagree intelligently so they can really be friends later on?

CHAPTER 17

How to Take a Son into the Business

How can a boy work for his father and the two of them get along?

That question comes often in my mail. And many of these queries are prompted by some negative history in the family, or a bad scene somewhere.

But now from Binghamton, New York, comes a three-page letter on "How to take a son into the business."

The writer is a third-generation president of this successful manufacturing concern. He has three teenage sons, all interested in joining him when they're ready.

Straight from where it's happening:

"From my own experience, if I were to give advice on how to take your son into business, it would go like this:

"1. Provide him with summer jobs in the business. Rough work. Ordinary work. Low wages. This will give him an idea of what the company is like from the bottom.

"2. Point out that the business will be successful only

as long as the people in it are competent. Therefore, if he's coming in, he'll need to be educated—competent.

"3. Adopt the policy that he should work somewhere else before he comes here. Maybe two years. Maybe five.

"4. Make it clear to everyone in the business that the president's son will be treated like everyone else. No favors.

"5. At some point give him a chance to buy in. Don't give him an interest. Ownership will mean more if he pays for it.

"6. I would encourage him to become expert where I am weak. I'd let him know my weaknesses and show him how he could help the company by developing his own particular skills. Example: If my strong point is engineering, maybe he could develop expertise in marketing.

"7. I would always be ready to listen to his ideas, be open to his ingenuity, let him be creative. I would continually point out to him, and to others, places where he is helping make the company what all of us want it to be."

"Of course, all this takes time. It takes time to plan and explain, observe and guide. But if you knew the feeling between my sons and me and if you understood my feeling about my father, I think you would say it is worth everything which has gone into it."

Down underneath everything the man says, I hear this solid drum beat:

A father's job is not to make his children a success. It is to take the time and to prepare the way so they can make themselves successful.

CHAPTER 18

Doing It Our Way

He never played ball with his son. Didn't coach Little League. No fishing. No hunting. They didn't work on cars together, but they had a good thing going.

Today's account of good fathering is right out of a college bull session.

We'd been in that dormitory room a long time, rapping like crazy on their themes. It was getting late, but they seemed in no hurry, so I asked a question.

There's a lull sometimes in a bull session when it's good to change the subject. Since it really was my turn, I told them about "Strictly for Dads." Would they mind kicking this gong around?

They not only didn't mind, they tied right into it. The athletic bit came in for a lot of recall. A place kicker (turned out he was the best ever in their school) described how his dad had him kicking before he started first grade. Same thing from some baseball players, a golfer or two, and one of the stars on their tennis team.

Another dad was an auctioneer. He trained his son to be one of his bid takers, how to handle livestock, keep records, recognize value. Then his dad died, but the boy is making his way through school on what he learned. Three nights each week he does his thing at the sales barn.

Then there was this different-looking character who didn't say thing one until all the others had made their contribution. Now he broke loose, and what a story. He explained how he and his dad had read together since he was very small. Mythology, classics, poets, the master novelists, science-fiction, mystery, the works. Then with deep emotion, he added this line which got us all right here, "My father was a cripple."

So many things I wish I could do. I watch other dads and think sometimes, "I'd like to teach my boys to fix cars, throw curves, shoot in the low seventies." But that's not me.

Wonder if I should quit worrying about what I can't do. Maybe the secret is to stop focusing on my short-comings and do what I *can* do as a dad.

CHAPTER 19

Time for Hostility

"Shut up, both of you, that's enough!"

Words of one dad, with a most unusual technique for handling hostility.

At their house they call this father's idea, "Wednesday Night Is Mad Night." It started one evening when he came home tired from the office. As he opened the door, he heard his teenage daughter having it out with her mom, both yelling full volume.

"I'd had all I could take that day," he said. "So I yelled at the top of *my* lungs, 'Shut up, you two, that's enough!' Then I cut a hole in the top of a box and issued this edict, 'From now on, any time anyone has a gripe, write it out, drop it in the box and we'll discuss it Wednesday.' Of course, some battles do have to be settled right now. But it's funny how this goes. Sometimes by Wednesday we can't even remember what it was about. Or if we do remember, it seems kind of silly. If you haven't tried it, don't knock it. I tell you, with us it's made a big difference."

There are many ways to handle hostility. In some families the rule is "bury it. Push it down inside. Forget it." But suppose it doesn't forget us?

Open a magazine, read the newspaper, turn on T.V. Obviously, some of the young have never been trained to let off steam in a sensible way. It it because they weren't allowed to surface their feelings at home?

Here's a letter with an unusual tribute. It's from a college girl saying, "The most loving thing I think my parents ever did for me was to let me hate them when I felt like it. Know what I mean? Not real hate, maybe, but real anger."

That could be worth a retake. Are we operating under the delusion that our children ought to like us all the time? Would it improve things around here if we could be loving enough to let them surface their negatives thoroughly?

"Wednesday night is mad night" does have an unusual sound. But for better fathering (mothering too) couldn't it be a good thing?

CHAPTER 20

"Say It Back"

"I just hate my math teacher. She doesn't explain one thing. I think she's stupid."

Sally talking, telling it like it is from her viewpoint. Sally is fifteen and a high school sophomore.

Now, what will we answer Sally?

If you're like most of us, you're tempted to say the wrong thing. You may take up for the teacher: "Sally, you know that's not true. She wouldn't be teaching if she was stupid." (Really? How can we be sure? It's been some time since we were in school. And some teachers who are book-brilliant are not real bright at handling people.)

Or we might say, "I had a few teachers like that too, Sally." (Which misses the point again. Sally isn't looking for sympathy. Right now she could care less how we had it.)

Or maybe we mount the pulpit and preach a little, "Well, if you children would all be more respectful, your teacher might do better." (The final cut-off. From here, it's downhill all the way.)

What Sally really wants from us is something else. She'd like us to listen long enough for her to vent her frustration. Psychologists talk about "listening with the third ear." What they're saying is that it isn't enough to hear voices. We must also get meanings.

So how? One answer is "Say it back." In "say it back" we simply repeat what the other person has said. We may alter it a bit, put it in our own words, add a little. When Sally says, "I hate my math teacher. I think she's stupid," we say it back like this:

"You mean you don't like your math teacher. She doesn't make things clear. You think she's not very bright."

This paves the way for Sally to go on with her true feelings. "Yeah. She gives the dumbest tests. I made sixty-seven today. I just know I'll get a big fat 'F' for the whole crummy course."

Now Sally is beginning to surface what's really troubling her. She isn't doing well. She's afraid. At this moment her only need is to get her true feelings up front, where she can see them and we can.

One father who worked on this till he mastered it, said, "When I quit moralizing, I was amazed how the kids kept talking until they had worked out their own solutions."

Question: Would I be a better dad if I'd button my lip more often and "listen with the third ear"?

CHAPTER 21

A Trip to the Bluff

"Dear Dr. Shedd:

"Would you like to know a little thing any father can do to help his children over the rough places?

"I grew up in Iowa and played girls' basketball. Girls' basketball is a big thing in Iowa. Because I was tall, I led our team in scoring from my sophomore year on. I got a lot of publicity and was mentioned for All-State. But in my sophomore and junior years I didn't make it. That nearly killed me, because I had my heart set on going to a particular small college which was always in competition for the collegiate championship. Because I didn't make it both of those years, I was way down and must have been awful to live with.

"One night at dinner my father said, 'Ruby, I think you need a trip to the bluff.' Of course, I knew what that meant. Overlooking the Mississippi River, there is a high bluff where our family would go picknicking. Up there you can see for miles and miles. You can also see the farms, the green fields, cows and horses grazing, some little towns and big ones. Plus the river winding forever. You can even see three states.

"So each of those years my father took me on a Saturday to the bluff. We packed a picnic and when we got there, he left me alone for a while just to look.

"Do you understand what I am talking about? When you are troubled and way down, you think that your problem is the only thing.

"But way up high, somehow, you get a different perspective and the bigness of things makes your troubles seem smaller. This is especially true if you are religious.

"My husband and I do this same thing with our children and without exception it has always worked.

"I thought maybe there might be other fathers who could use this idea because it is so great to have a father who will take the time to help you when you are down.

"P.S. You will be interested to know that when I was a senior, I did make All-State and went to the college of my choice."

CHAPTER 22

Listen! Concentrate!

"Dear Dr. Shedd:

"Can you tell me why our kids clam up when they reach their teens? Now it's Wendy, and I was sure she'd never be like that. Wendy has been nothing but fun. But this year she just goes in her room and shuts the door. When we ask her questions, all we get is sounds from far away. Are there things a parent can do to keep the roads open?"

Yes, I think there are.

Nobody knows all there is to know about teenagers, but I know this: with mine, things always go better if I remember two words.

LISTEN and *CONCENTRATE*

When they start talking, button your lip, Charlie. Right now what they need is an ear to pound, a place to mumble, whisper, get mad, let it all out.

Listen. Listen. Listen.

Then, concentrate!

Meaning? Do your very best to pick up on the feelings behind the words. I need this reminder. It is so easy to tune in for a few minutes, few seconds, then with so many things on the mind, drift away.

Concentrate. Concentrate. Concentrate.

Awesome call! But it can be done and some dads do it. Here's one paragraph from a junior high girl:

"The thing I appreciate most about my dad is that he will always take the time to listen. I mean even when he's tired, he does. He never makes fun of anything I say, and he always tries real hard to understand what I am telling him. You know there are not many people like this, especially parents. So do you know what happens? A lot of my girl friends come over and talk to my father all the time too. I think it is so great to have a dad like that."

CHAPTER 23

Hmmmmm . . .

"Dear Dr. Shedd:

"Do you know what I think makes the difference between good parents and the other kind? I think it is mostly that the good parents will listen. Mine will, and that's what I appreciate most about them. They don't listen just for words, but they also listen to what my sister and I are trying to say. You know what I mean, the way we really feel."

That must be another thing the psychologists mean by "listening with the third ear."

And this is not something we luck into. It's an art to be learned. So I'd like to pass along one simple expression which has helped when I remember to use it.

This is the plain little sound, "Hmmmmm . . ."

"Hmmmmm . . ." can convey many messages. It may be saying, "I'm interested. Keep talking."

Or "I'm getting skeptical. Pitch me a little harder. I'm still open."

Or again it can shade off with that beautiful special message, "I'm getting a glimmer. Flash me some more."

Now and then some dad calls long distance. It happened again the other day. Said he was having a problem with one of his boys. But I don't think the call was worth his money, because I could hardly get a word in edgewise. Like Tennyson's brook he went babbling on forever.

When he hung up, I couldn't help wondering, Is that his problem with the boy? If the poor kid felt like I did, it could be!

Question with whammy:

Do my children ever feel that way about me?

"Hmmmmm . . ."

CHAPTER 24

Discover Iowa

"Dear Dr. Shedd:

"From some of the things you say in your column, I thought you might be able to help me. I have been offered a job with a new company. It is a wonderful opportunity and something I've always wanted. But if I take it, that would mean we will have to move to another state. It seems like so many people we know have trouble with their children after they move, especially teenagers.

"Do you know any families who moved and they didn't have trouble? Also if they didn't, can you tell us what they did to keep their family together?"

Important question, and from here the answer is "Yes. It can be done! I know many families who have moved successfully."

"Dear Dr. Shedd:

"When we read your column on moving, we thought maybe you'd like to hear about us. Last year we came here after living all our lives in Illinois. My husband is a trucker, so he has a chance to see a lot of places when he is going around. He looks for things our family might like. Then on Sundays we pack a picnic and take off.

"We have visited forts, and zoos, and Air Force bases, amusement parks and rivers for boating and fishing. We've gone to state fairs, harness racing, flea markets, and last week we saw a fantastic collection of old clocks.

"Everyone in the family seems to be crazy about this. Even our teenagers will ask, 'Where are we going this weekend?' We call it our 'discover Iowa program,' and every time we come back from one of these trips, it seems like we belong a little bit more. But my husband and I feel sure what our children like most about this is just that we're with each other all that much."

Two good clues here for successful moving:

1. Have fun;
2. Make it a time for togetherness.

And how about a special pat on the back for a special dad? He has to be very special, traveling all week in a truck and then going some more on weekends for the good of his family.

CHAPTER 25

Preventive Fun

Phyllis makes me think of that beautiful old compliment, "The only unhappiness she ever causes is to be absent from the meeting."

One day I asked this souped-up lover of everyone and everything, "Whatever happened to turn out a girl like you?"

Answer, strictly for dads—

Very early she said her folks gave her the idea that life was for having fun. Sure, it was for lots of other things. Serious and semiserious too, but never overserious. Whatever else, this old world was to be enjoyed. And that was interesting, because I happen to know they were poor, real poor. Lots of kids on a scrubby farm, all of them pitching in to keep some groceries on the table. Scrabbling to eke out an existence. Yet they still had fun.

How? Here's one way.

"Well, mostly I think it was my dad and some of the

special things he did. Like every spring he'd take off two or three days from his job in town to help us dam the creek. You remember our swimming hole. We built it every spring, and talk about fun! All of our cousins would come from everywhere, and the neighbor kids, they'd come, and our friends. Now we all knew that dad needed his job in town, because he couldn't pay the bills without it. So taking off time was a very serious thing. But dad was also serious about fun. I mean fun was real important to him. I suppose it was important for a lot of reasons, but when I think back, I guess this must be one of them— When we were in high school some of the kids in our town got in trouble. I mean they got in trouble with the law. Big trouble. A whole bunch of them were in on it. But do you suppose it was just an accident that not one of our family, our cousins, our neighbors or any of the kids who were in on my dad's fun ever got in trouble?"

CHAPTER 26

The Straight Skinny by Eleven

Panic from the father front.

Paragraph number one of a long letter:

"Dear Dr. Shedd:

"No way to tell you how shook up I am. Last night when I got home, my wife handed me the enclosed note. She found it in Debby's room. And would you believe Debby is only eleven? Where could she have learned such filthy language? And does she really know what it means? For God's sake, can you tell us what to do?"

Yes, I can tell you what to do, or I can tell you what I'd do. Fast.

I'd get Debby out of the house alone. I'd take her for a hamburger. Pizza. Coke. I'd do this so we could have absolute privacy, no interruptions, total attention.

(Incidentally, I wouldn't say thing one about her note. It *is* hers, you know. Or it *was*. Females of any age build up awful things about other females snooping in private papers.)

Now I'd deliver the message right out of my father's heart. I'd give her "the straight skinny." That's what the kids call it, meaning plain unvarnished fact. I'd start with the fact of facts, that sex is beautiful, because God made it that way. I'd tell her this is the way it is with her parents, and I hope that some day she and the man she loves will feel like we do.

I'd give her the straight skinny too on the words, right terminology for sex organs, sex acts. I would also go over the wrong words and what they mean. I'd explain what's normal sex, what isn't. Perversion, distortion, all of it. I'd clue this little girl in totally. I'd try to give her everything she might need for coping with reality.

Why shouldn't her mother take on this assignment? Haven't mothers always talked to their daughters, female to female? Isn't that the best way?

Answer: "No!" Ours is a new day. Patterns of child development are fast changing, and we need to reckon with these changes. One change is that preteen girls are not very high on their mother. But to most girls this age, dad is beginning to look better all the time. Circumstances have moved the scenery inside a preteenager and father is coming center stage. Anything he says has more chance of coming through.

Debby is only eleven and I'm betting she doesn't know what she's writing. Let's hope she's only getting it down so she can see what it looks like. Maybe an ego trip, straining to be a big girl. Of course, nobody knows for sure about Debby. But this is certainly true, she didn't get what she needed when she needed it.

Can we give them too much too soon?

I don't think so. The good Lord has put His children together with an amazing inside computer and it works like this:

> If we give them the beautiful in love
> And make it the total package;
> If they don't need it yet,
> They will file it away in their inside computer.
> Then when the negative comes,
> They have something positive to meet it.
> And often the most positive info
> Is "the straight skinny"
> From a caring dad.

CHAPTER 27

How Far Can I Go and Still Be Safe?

"Daddy, how far can a girl go and still be safe?"

Unusual question from a teenage girl to her father, but this was an unusual girl. Of course, I would think so. Any dad tends to believe his own daughter is unusual.

The reason she would ask me is that we had been going out together once each month from the time she was two. Dinner, shopping, a show, the beach.

So there we were eating in our favorite fish house and she was asking, "How far can a girl go and still be safe?" No use getting academic with questions like, "What do you mean, safe?" I knew what she meant and so did she. So do thousands of teenagers in high school and college who ask the same question: "If we don't want to get over-involved, where should we stop?"

Plain vanilla question from the youth front deserving a plain vanilla answer. And the plainest vanilla answer I know is:

"Hands outside the clothes."

Many fathers tell me they freeze when it comes to sex talk. I understand. Most of us have hangups which tend to leave us tongue-tied. But we better get over it. Today's kids need all the help they can get. And in the ideal family dad takes the lead with sex education.

Do we really want our children to get their training from the ill-informed, the sick, the negative? If we don't do our job, that's where they'll get it. Pornography is everywhere and so is dirty sex. The banal, the bawdy create a fallout of confusion and plain old-fashioned evil.

When it comes to sex education, straight talk from somewhere has always been a major need. Some of us didn't get it where we should have gotten it, and where any child should get it first is at home. On the level, in love, plain vanilla.

Plain vanilla question: "How far can a girl go and still be safe?"

Plain vanilla answer: "Hands outside the clothes."

CHAPTER 28

Dirty Humor

The home in which I grew up was across the street from a log cabin grocery. It was the village meeting place. Our town crones would gather there for bringing each other up to date on the latest of everything. What the weather was going to do. Old Bill's recent antics. News from the night cop. "Did you hear about John's boy getting promoted?" "Did you know about the fire at Janesville?" The most recent word on certain widows. All these with laughing, shaking of heads, and some things whispered.

Then there was this one man who always had a risque story for everything. You name a topic. He could color it ever so slightly, add some double entendre, sex it up. Some of his contributions were plain funny. But it was plain too that he often left his audience embarrassed. Turned off.

I was only a boy when I heard all this and observed these variant reactions; and I remember clearly one thing

Ike said. Ike was the storekeeper. He worked for Mr. Lowry who owned a lot of things in our town. Gentle person, Ike. Ideal for any job with people. It would be very unusual for Ike to say anything negative about anyone. That's why I remember the day when the man with the dirty mind had been especially vulgar. He'd left the store now. And Ike said out loud, "Do you know what I think? I don't think the poor guy is getting any."

Maybe Ike didn't know that I didn't know what he was talking about then. But I do remember what he said. Knowing what I know now, I think he may have zeroed in on the problem.

Is there any boy anywhere who doesn't need some help toward understanding dirty humor? Or any daughter? Only one answer to that question, and it's one more place where a caring dad can make all the difference.

I want my children to enjoy sex. So do you. We want them to enjoy it so much they can laugh about it when it's funny. But we also want them to know that smudge on the surface probably comes from smudge inside. And if we go at it right, they will take it from a dad who cares enough to put it to them straight— *Sex is too good to be cheapened with negative talk.*

The West Point cadets have a prayer worth any father's pondering. Could be just the thing for our children too:

"Lord, if I can't be funny and clean,
    help me to just be clean."

CHAPTER 29

She Was a Tramp, Almost

She was a tramp. Almost. That's what she said. And the reason she could say "almost" was her dad.

What would you do if your daughter was a tramp, almost? I'd probably run the emotional gamut. Disappointment. Worry. Anger. Embarrassment.

No doubt her dad went through all these, but then he did another thing. He sat down with her for a heart to heart talk and this is her report:

"Dear Dr. Shedd:

"I'd like to nominate my father for 'One Neat Dad,' because looking back, I think he is the reason why I can be proud of myself today. I am about to finish nurse's training and when I look back I realize how different it could have been. When I started high school, everything went wrong. I got in with the wrong crowd and thought I was so smart. The truth is I was a tramp. Almost.

"It was then my father sat me down and had a long talk

69

with me. What he told me was how proud he was to be married to a real lady. He said most men feel like that, and then he said he hoped some day I would be married to a man who could be proud of me. He also talked about my having children and what it would mean to them to have a mother they could be proud of. He didn't scold or threaten me or put me down. He just talked quiet and in fact, he was so great that I believe this is what really made me change.

"Some of my friends got into bad trouble and I know it could have been me. Now I am engaged to a wonderful man and all of this is why I think my father is one neat dad."

Really is, isn't he?

Great question for any father to lay on his children:

"What kind of person will you be five years from now? Ten? What are you doing today and how will that look when you have a family of your own?"

CHAPTER 30

Two Dads in the Garden

"Same fire hardens the egg and melts the butter."

It's an ancient saying worth pondering, but sometimes whether it hardens or softens depends on dad.

Two letters. First, from a hurting mother:

"Maybe you could write someday on fathers who ride their hobbies too hard. My husband is big on gardening. We live in the city and he has a plot out in the country. We also have four children, and he has absolutely destroyed their feelings for him by insisting that they learn how to garden.

"Maybe it wouldn't be so bad if he wasn't such a perfectionist. With him, everything has to be done exactly so and he goes literally out of his mind when it isn't. I try not to get too involved, but when I see the children gradually turning away from him, it is almost more than I can bear. When should a mother speak up? I ask myself—is it when a man's garden means more than his children?"

71

On and on for several pages she describes the total turn-off of one dad whose plants mean more than his paternity.

Second letter from a daughter looking back:

"We all miss my dad, but I've enjoyed these weeks since his death, looking back to all the things he taught me. And do you know what I remember most? It's those hours we spent in the garden. When I was little, he taught me how to plant, to fertilize, to water, and cultivate, but that isn't all. He gave me so much of his wonderful philosophy while we were out there hoeing together.

"I work in personnel, and you wouldn't know how many times I think back to things my dad said. Like when there was a weed growing too close to a plant, he would say, 'Jeannie, you'd better let it grow. You'd lose too much if you took it out.' I think a father can do so much with his hobby if he uses it right with his children, don't you?"

Sure do. And even if gardening isn't my thing, I might do well to check this out—

Are there any places where I'm putting "things" ahead of my fathering?

CHAPTER 31

My Pop's Tops

What will your children remember about you?

Some years ago a newspaper ran an interesting Father's Day contest in which children were to write essays on "My Pop's Tops." (Sorry, I don't know the name of the paper, nor the name of the small boy winner.) But here is his prize entry.

"We have so much fun with my dad that I wisht I had known him sooner. He is a farmer. He smells like a cow, and when I smell that cow in the house, I know Pop is home and I am glad.

"My pop's tops because every time I ast for a knickel he will start preeching that when he was a boy he had to earn his knickels, and at the same time he is putting his hand in his pocket and pulls out a knickel for me.

"My pop's tops because he was a brave soldier. He didn't see me till I was three years old, yet he is just as good to me as if he knew me all my life."

Well, that *is* a winner, isn't it?

Wouldn't any dad like his children saying, "My pop's tops." But doing a retake on his essay, it's evident this little guy was judging his dad by the common everyday things. A smell, a nickel, the feeling inside.

Do we tend sometimes to overconcern ourselves with deals like food, shelter, clothing, and the strong protector bit?

Sure, these are important. I want to be a good provider. So do you. But really! Does anything matter more than living so our children could say,

"We have so much fun with my dad, I wisht I had known him sooner."

CHAPTER 32

Chop a Little Wood for the Next Fellow

"What do you remember most about your father?"

I recently asked a group of men that question and the results surprised me.

Almost without exception the most-remembered items were little things. A few big deals, but not many. More often they were small moments, small bits of advice, small sayings.

One such is the theme of this interesting letter. The writer is a newly retired grandfather reflecting back to his own boyhood.

"Every year my dad would take me on a hunting trip up into the north country. Far back into the woods. We would canoe part of the way, then backpack to a secluded cabin. Every year we would get our limit of game, because very few people made it so far back. But if you ask what I remember most, it wasn't what you might think. It wasn't all those deer, the bobcat, the wolves, or even that special year we got a moose.

"What I remember most is how we always chopped wood before we left our campsite. Of course, the first time I commented in the negative. We were tired, we were leaving, so why chop wood? That's when my father said this thing I've never forgotten. In fact, it made such an impression on me it actually became kind of a life motto. Just one short sentence to live by and this is it: 'Chop a little wood for the next fellow.'

"Come to think of it, it does seem rather odd that out of all those great times we had up there, this is what I remember most!"

Next time you're with the young set ask some questions and how is this for starters? "What do you think you'll remember most about your dad?"

And what will my children remember most about me? Something big? Little? Negative? Positive? Or maybe something as old-shoe as "Chop a little wood for the next fellow."

CHAPTER 33

Making Friends with the Darkness

Paul and Mercedes are among the beautiful people. They're very good to look at, especially Mercedes. But some of the things they do with their family make them extra beautiful.

For instance, if you rode past their house on a starlit night, you might see an unusual thing. They're sitting on that little front patio, talking about the North Star, the Big Dipper, the Milky Way. They are having a family discussion on wonders in the night sky.

Experts say that what a child thinks of the dark could make a terrific difference. Why? One psychologist says: "The fewer false fears a child brings into adulthood, the more successful he will be."

The man doesn't say what he means by "success," but whatever he means, his words are right on target for any parent. Maybe those little things like bedtime rituals accomplish more than anyone knows.

Floyd and Jean have an interesting version all their own. Floyd is a big worker at the Boys' Club. He has a chance to observe the young close up and he knows how they think. So he worked out a little game for his family. They don't play it every night, just whenever they think someone needs it. They call it, "Now we're going to tell what we're afraid of." Floyd shares something the little ones can understand. Jean does too. Then each of the children takes a turn. They say, "You wouldn't believe the things which frighten children, and how close we feel when we discuss our fears together."

That too heavy for your tribe at night? Might be. But don't scrub it too soon because it's the unshared fears which make things scary any time, day or night.

This summer a lady in Vermont told us something about her dad we really liked. We were sitting by her picture window looking down the valley. It was storming when she told us this. Dark clouds, heavy rain, wind blowing, deep thunder, and lightning off in the distance.

We were all quiet as we watched. Then she said quietly:

"I can still remember when I was a little girl.

"My father would hold me on his knees, and we'd look out the window while he told me all about the rain and wind, thunder and lightning and the elements. Do you know I still like storms?"

What she meant by "still" is that she's now over eighty.

For at least seventy years, maybe seventy-five, she's been doing a recall on what her father said and all this time she's been liking storms.

Good question for dads:

What will my children remember about me when they're eighty?

CHAPTER 34

Two Boy Drivers

How would you react to these letters?

"Dear Dr. Shedd:

"My wife and I are having an argument which we can't seem to settle. She agreed that I should write to you and we would go by whatever you say. Our son, Donny, is fourteen. All his life he has been inordinately interested in cars. In our state they don't get driver's permits until sixteen. He is literally straining at the leash. Last week he slipped out in the night, took our station wagon and fortunately backed into the neighbor's mailbox on the way out. I use the word 'fortunately' because we heard it so we could stop him. I say we ought to lower the boom on him. I won't go into details, but where my wife and I disagree is the severity of punishment. What would you do if your fourteen-year-old boy had pulled a thing like that?"

The above is only one paragraph from a much longer letter. And here's one answer straight from the parent front:

"Dear Dr. Shedd:

"My husband is a beautiful father in so many ways. For example, Jimmy, who is thirteen, is absolutely crazy about cars. So my husband takes him to car shows, car races, and even lets him help fix little things on our pickup. Recently he has been taking Jimmy on Sunday afternoons to the church parking lot and teaching him how to drive. Jimmy is so serious about it all, my husband says he knows it will make him a better driver. But I tell him that isn't the only thing. What Jimmy thinks of his father is beautiful, too."

I can see a barrage of letters coming. "It's illegal," "a form of dishonesty," "he's teaching his son to be disrespectful of the law."

I showed these two letters to a highway patrolman friend of mine and asked him, "What do you think?"

From the man with the badge:

"If any father asks me whether he should teach his son to drive on an empty parking lot before he's driver's license age, I'd tell him that's what I'm doing with my son."

CHAPTER 35

He Specializes in Little People

He specializes in little people's stuff. Games, stories, imaginary playmates, bedtime tales with sound effects.

His wife says he's unique. She labels him one of a kind.

"My husband is undoubtedly among the best with small children I have ever seen. Our sons are five, three, and two. Anyone who can get small boys to sit still very long has to be unique. Yet our sons will sit for a long time and listen to their dad's stories and absorb every word. They also like to add their ideas to the story and he encourages them. Sometimes he incorporates the boys' names in his story and he adds sound effects like crinkling paper for a fire burning. His creation of imaginary friends for them has also given them the desire to be creative.

"Yet it isn't all stories. Sometimes he goes into his act and becomes a talking Dumbo clown giving free rides. Or he is a wicked witch making some special potion. Then they taste this pretend mixture and see who can make the funniest faces. Sometimes they chase each other around the house like frogs and my husband adds the sound. Another thing they play is race cars. Each one has his own imaginary car and they take turns winning the race.

"You can see why I say my husband is unique. You can also understand why he has a big following with the little people in our neighborhood. Do you know what I think? I think children outside our family are so fond of him partially because he is taking the place of their father. That's true of too many, and I think it's sad."

Question: If I would take the time to unbend a little, could I do a better job at home? So, making up stories and acting the clown isn't my thing? This much foolishness is not for me?

Wonder if the Lord had any special father-meaning in mind when He said, "Unless you become as little children, you shall not enter the kingdom of heaven."

CHAPTER 36

Miss Thelma

What difference does it make whether a dad is accessible to his children?

For one answer meet Miss Thelma. She's a good friend of ours; a retired school teacher, getting well down the road now. She's at that age when there isn't much else to do but sit and reminisce. ·

So we listen. We listen as she tells us about her girlhood; about the antebellum home where she grew up; about the fine finishing schools she attended. Often this background will produce a genuine lady, and that's what it did for Miss Thelma. But she's very lonesome.

So why didn't she marry? Even today she looks like a good bet for somebody's trip to the altar. But in her own words, "I had all the beaus any girl would want, but when they began to get serious somehow I couldn't go on."

If you could hear her tell about her father, you'd say, "Here's one clue." She idolized the man. For her, he was the epitome. Only he was so distant, so remote. Then in typical Miss Thelma generosity, she says, "I know he must have had problems which made him that way. But I honestly think the distance between us when I was little affected me all my life."

Strange! From a background like that one girl will get involved with men. This one lets herself go too much, too soon; but that one builds walls to protect herself.

Some people call Miss Thelma an old maid, set in her ways, odd. But if you knew her like we know her, you would say, "She's beautiful." And I think you might also be musing—

Isn't she one more answer to the question:

"What difference does it make whether a father is accessible to his children?"

CHAPTER 37

Should This Man Marry?

Should this man marry? He's engaged to a woman with two daughters, very fond of the lady, and he likes her girls. But he wonders how much the girls will like him.

"Dear Dr. Shedd:

"Can you give me some advice on becoming a good stepfather? Barb has two girls, eleven and eight. I get along especially well with the youngest, but I see warning signs ahead with the other one.

"Maybe the reason I am hesitating is that my sister married after she had been widowed. Her children are high schoolers now and for almost five years I've watched their stepfather struggle with it. Of course, I don't know all the details, but I think he's given it a real try and my sister agrees he has. Yet somehow he and the children have never developed an effective relationship.

"Barb and I have a great thing going, but believe me, if I had to go through what my sister's husband has gone through, I wouldn't want any part of that. What do you think?"

Let's start with the hopeful note. My mail brings numerous letters from stepchildren. Almost all of these express their gratitude. Sure, the others don't write. But I do know this straight from where it's happening—stepfathers can and often do win the love of their stepchildren.

All over this land there are second-hand sons and daughters with high praise for the man who came along when they needed him.

Recently I heard a psychologist say, "Generally, successful parenting is more attitudinal than biological." Which being interpreted means, good fathering comes from the heart.

And almost without exception when a stepchild sends accolades for his stepfather, the tribute includes these items:

"He listens. . . .We do things together. . . .He spends time with me. . . .I get the feeling he really cares."

CHAPTER 38

Quality, not Quantity!

Bud is plant manager for a paper company. Big job. He never knows when the phone will ring calling him back to the mill. "This mixture needs checking." "That blankety-blank machine broke down again." "We've got a leak here."

Bud is crazy about his work. He likes machines, he likes men, and he especially likes the feeling that somebody needs him. So he goes.

But then there's Dick, and does Bud ever like Dick! Dick is eight. So what can a dad with a job like that do about his eight-year old? This is Bud's answer, and I think it's a winner:

"I simply don't have the energy to spend hours with Dick. So I make up for it with shorty periods of concentrated time. Almost every day, or at least several times each week, we have little fifteen-minute periods which are Dick's time with me, and my time with him.

Man to man, just the two of us together. He tells me what he's been thinking. I tell him something I think he'd like to know. Maybe we just play catch or eat a snack together. Or I look at his rock collection.

"Since we started this, I've come up with a whole new thought for me. It isn't the *amount* of time I spend with my family. It's the *kind* of time that counts."

Paul does it another way. He's an addict. Football, baseball, basketball, track, hockey, the works. And he says:

"I'm not going to let my addiction come between me and my kids. Any time I'm reading the paper and one of them comes in the room, I put the paper down, and give them a chance to say something if they want to. Or I ask a question. Anything to let them know I'm ready.

"I read somewhere, 'There never *has* been anything in the newspaper; there never *will* be anything in the paper; and there's nothing in today's paper as important as my kids.' "

Question: What takes place in the mind of the child when his dad has time for him?

I think the answer is that we bring out the best in people when we let them know they are important.

So here's a tip of the hat to Bud, and another in Paul's direction. Two smart dads, each in his own way remembering:

> "A Dad Is for Spending Time With."

CHAPTER 39

Handling Jealousy
Before It Arrives

Wherever two or three children are gathered together, there will be jealousy in the midst of them.

Standard equipment on brothers and sisters. Sure thing, too, from sister to sister or brother to brother.

What can we do with rivalry?

At our house jealousy is handled better if we attack it before it arrives, meaning we have some built-in jealousy preventives.

For starters, there is the simple little business of assigning different bedtimes, depending on age. As a child grows older, he stays up later. The fourth grader goes to bed earlier than his junior high brother. Sure, he doesn't like it, but it hurts less if he knows that at junior high age, he'll have the same hours.

Another big help has been increasing allowances as each child grows older. This means turning over more and more of the child's expenditures to himself; allowing him to use his funds with less supervision; telling the young ones they will have the same rights at the same age. This too can be a big assist.

Naturally, the same thing goes for responsibilities. As privileges increase, duties increase too.

But for us this is the biggest help and it is called "Time out alone with dad." What this means is that each child has at least one date per month with his father. No interference, no interruption, no exception. This is one-on-one time for each son, each daughter. Dinner, lunch, breakfast, ball game, movie, shopping, concert, miscellany.

More than anything this is the super mitigator for that "life isn't fair" feeling. And that isn't all. One of the greatest side benefits is a father's discovery month by month, year by year, that his children are fine people. Sorted out from the crowd at home, they come through loud and clear as individuals worth knowing one on one.

CHAPTER 40

Sibling Rivalry

Anne Louise gave her little brother away last week. It was the talk of the town. The whole neighborhood had a lot of fun with it. But it also made some of us do a retake.

Anne Louise is five and her baby brother is three months. On this particular day her mother went to the crib and found the baby wasn't there. Of course, she panicked. But to cut across the hysteria, Anne Louise had wrapped him up nicely and carried him three doors down the street to the Jacksons'. Then she made a speech about what a fine boy he was but they didn't want him any more. They had all decided things would be better if he lived with the Jacksons from now on.

Bernice Jackson is one of those wonderfully sensitive people so she fell right in with it. As soon as Anne Louise had gone, she made a phone call to report the baby safe at her house:

Well, it was one of those days to remember and laugh

about later. What's awful at the moment can be fun in the recall.

We've said it before—wherever two or three are gathered together there will be jealousy in the midst. That's particularly true at certain stages, certain years.

But at any stage it's tough stuff to handle. Which means smart parents keep their radar out, and when they hear the sounds of envy, they consider making changes. Changes like what? Like this straight from Anne Louise's mother:

"We decided she was trying to tell us something. Obviously, she liked it better when she had us alone. So what can we do? I decided one thing I can do is to ask her to help me more with the baby. I'll give her some responsibility, let her get closer to him herself."

And this from her dad:

"No question what I need to do. I need to spend more time with Anne Louise."

CHAPTER 41

Private Time

They call it "private time," and it's always done in the little room right off their den. The door is closed now, and the reason? The reason is that dad and one of his daughters are having "private time."

Maybe they are discussing a problem. Something heavy. A friend hasn't been nice to her. Her sister is bugging her. Her mother is so hard to understand.

So the young lady talks. She tells her father whatever she wants to tell. She asks questions. He listens. They discuss. Then they work out some answers. Share some secrets. And they laugh.

How long are they at it? Straight from where it's happening, this report strictly for dads:

"It's amazing how little time this takes. Usually, it's only a few minutes. I think what they care about most is that they can be alone with their dad, completely alone. But sometimes I wonder if they aren't learning some other valuable things. Like how to carry on discussions with a man. They're sure going to need that someday. And I'm learning some things too. For instance, I've always had this tendency to come up with answers too fast. That's the way I am. So it's good for me when I have to put on the brakes and listen. I think it even helps me at the office.

"Anyway I thought maybe you'd like to know about 'private time.'

"P.S. I forgot to tell you the girls are five and three."

CHAPTER 42

Dad on a Low Stool

"Dear Dr. Shedd:

"We have a three-year-old and we always pay special attention when your columns are about small children. Recently you said that it sometimes works to get down on the floor and look them right in the eye.

"We are using a variation of this which my wife and I thought might be helpful to other readers.

"Because Tricia is the kind who communicates her intense feelings, I decided to try your eyeball-to-eyeball suggestion. What I did was to build a little stool for my wife and me to sit on when we need to talk to her straight.

"That stool idea was an immediate hit with Tricia, and actually, there has been less need for any kind of serious correction since we began using it. It is as though talking things out on her level makes her much nicer to live with.

"You might be interested also to know there are even times when she goes and gets the stool and brings it to one of us as an indicator she has something to discuss."

Straight from where it's happening, one little girl and two wise parents meeting each other on common ground.

Not long ago we went to a concert where we had to sit on the front row as part of an overflow crowd. In spite of a first-rate performance, those two hours of neck craning and head tilting were anything but first rate.

Maybe that's one reason this father's letter caught my eye. I wonder if constantly looking up day after day, month after month, might be one reason why the two-to-four period has been called "the worst age of man."

Excuse me while I go build a low stool.

CHAPTER 43

Strange World of Money Talk

Every dad should sit on the floor now and then and take a look at the world from down below. I've been recommending this since I saw the baby's dinner from that position. He had thrown his spoon on the floor, and this time I had to go under the table to retrieve it.

As I came up, I caught a glimpse of his food from *his* eye level. No doubt about it, from down here, those mashed potatoes looked like a great white mountain.

The other evening we heard a child psychologist, and some of the things we heard brought back memories of those mashed potatoes. His subject was "The Strange World of Money Talk to Small Ears." I believe he was quoting some unknown author with this classic:

"References to money popped up all over Jimmy's world, so slowly but surely he collected an odd, yet unrelated set of facts and fancies. He learned that money doesn't grow on trees. He heard that a $10 bill simply

97

melts away; that money has a way of slipping through fingers or burnings holes in pockets.

"Then suddenly he wondered whether anyone would object to his taking money which they had 'poured down rat holes.' But where was the rat hole?

"The shadow of money hung over Jimmy's playmates too. Grandmother said Alice had been 'born with a silver spoon in her mouth.' Maryanne's mother was 'poor as a church mouse.' Billy was pitied because his family lived 'over their heads.' Whenever Jimmy had even a penny of his own, he would clutch it tightly, remembering that Aunt Anna was forever saying, 'A fool and his money are soon parted.' "

As I pondered the man's presentation, what he said opened up new areas for sympathy. So much of our adult world must be dreadfully confusing to little children, unless, of course, they're getting help from someone, somewhere.

Where am I doing what needs doing to unconfuse my children's world?

Sure it takes time to think some of these hard things through, to see life from a child's viewpoint. But could this be another thing the small boy meant when he said,
"A Dad Is for Spending Time With."

CHAPTER 44

When There Are Other Demands

He's a doctor in Texas. On Father's Day last year his daughter wrote him a letter, the kind of letter any dad would like from his daughter. And when he sent me a copy of her letter, he wrote this personal letter to give me some of the background:

"Dear Dr. Shedd:

"I read your column regularly and I just have to share a letter with you. It came on Father's Day and if I live to be one hundred, this will always be one of the biggest thrills of my life.

"I'm a doctor and you know the old story. A plumber's faucets always leak, a painter's house is never painted, the electrician's lights won't turn on.

"Well, when we began our family, I decided early that I wanted to be a good father even more than I wanted to be a good doctor. So no matter how many calls I get; no matter how many other demands on my time; no matter what I'm doing, I always try to stop anything if I possibly can and give my children full attention.

"For example a few months ago my daughter had a particularly severe heartbreak. I heard her crying. I had been called to the hospital, but I knew she needed me too.

"So I went to her and put my arm around her and kept it around her for twenty minutes. Never said a word. Just sat there with my arm around her."

Now this one line from his daughter's letter:

"Dad, I think the thing I appreciate most about you is that I know you are my friend, because a friend will put you first even when they are busy with other things."

Maybe that one line should go on a card. Maybe I should put it up in my car where I can see it at a red light. Or on the mirror when I shave.

"A friend will put you first even when they are busy with other things."

CHAPTER 45

The Mayor Who Puts His Family First

He's the mayor and he's busy. Most mayors are busy. This one has thirty thousand people in his constituency. He says most of these citizens are fine folks, but then there are a few who give him fits. So he hears their complaints, makes decisions, takes his stand.

One of his recent stands says something strictly for dads. Every night at dinner, this mayor disconnects his phone. He knows people may be trying to reach him right now, but he wants to concentrate fully on his family. (Most public people know how it goes. The phone always rings at mealtime because that's a good bet to catch anyone home.)

Maybe no one would have known what was going on, except that the mayor's son gave it away. He's seven. His best friend is a seven-year-old girl and she happens to be the daughter of one of the councilmen.

When she took the story home, this councilman

understood now why he could never reach the mayor during dinner hour.

But since he isn't the mayor's biggest fan, he waited until town board meeting to bring it up.

Councilman: "Mr. Mayor, if there was an emergency during your dinner hour and you were needed, what would the citizens do? Let's say the town hall was on fire, and we couldn't reach you? What would you suggest, sir?"

Unfortunately, there was an inquisitive cub reporter present looking for Brownie points. Something controversial. Something exciting. So when he saw the possibilities here, he latched onto this like crazy, blew it all out of proportion.

That's why someone sent me the story and there was this paragraph which I think is a classic.

Quote from the mayor's answer:

"Yes, I suppose the city hall could catch on fire and if you see it, remember you'd only be wasting time trying to call me, because if it's during the dinner hour, my phone will be off the hook. So you come get me. But except for dire emergencies, let this be clearly understood: If our town needs a twenty-four-hour mayor, it better vote for somebody else at the next election. The present mayor happens to believe some things are more important than city business. And one such is the business of being alone with my family during dinner hour."

CHAPTER 46

Weekend Shrimper

George runs a shrimp boat off the East Coast. Since he works full time in a factory, he's only a weekend shrimper.

Nothing unusual about that, but in his story there is one unusual angle Strictly for Dads.

George first came to my attention when his eleven-year-old daughter nominated him in our One Neat Dad contest. She wrote a beautiful letter and after I heard her report I decided to get the full acount straight from the shrimper:

"Almost everybody these days can use some extra income. So that's how I got into shrimping. Six of us own the boat and my share isn't as big as the others. But I'm the only one with experience, so they give me a generous cut. There have always been shrimpers in our family, and I do know what I'm doing.

"Well, the reason my daughter wrote you is that I have

been going out weekends for the last two years. The fact is, it's never been so good. But one day I was sitting around during a lull, thinking. You can really think out there on the ocean. All of a sudden it hit me, 'You're making all this money and never seeing your family. You never play with the children, don't spend much time with your wife. They go to Mass without you, go to the boys' games without you, to the girls' recitals without you, and the truth is they're building a whole life without you.'

"I thought about that for several weeks and then I made a big decision. I decided that no matter how good business is, I'll settle for half as good and spend two weekends every month at home.

"You can bet when it came to my partners, this decision went over with a dull thud. So I told them if they couldn't live with it, I'd sell out my share. But they didn't take me up on it, and do you know what one of them said? He said, 'George, when you did that, I decided to have another look at my own life style and I want to thank you, because I needed to make some changes too.'"

So that's the story straight from George. You will remember we got into this, because his daughter says he's a winner.

Any dad is a winner who is willing to sacrifice some things to be at home more. Why? Because, once again, it's exactly like the young man says,

"A Dad Is for Spending Time With."

CHAPTER 47

Two Eds

This is the story of two Eds. They live in Fort Worth, and Ed, the younger, graduated last spring from Texas Tech. For a graduation present his father gave him a thirty-day trip by motorcycle. Across West Texas, New Mexico, Arizona, then up the California coast to Oregon. From there back home by way of Montana, North Dakota, Minnesota.

Sounds like fun for the boy, but the unusual feature here is that dad went along. Two motorcycles, a tent, bedrolls, cooking utensils, and various miscellany.

Here are a few words from Ed, the father:

"We cooked some of our own meals and camped out part of the time, stayed with friends and relatives along the way, and on occasion abandoned our tent for a motel room."

Ed Junior says,

"People thought we were brothers or just friends.

They'd say, 'You boys have a nice time now.' Well, we did. And it was a valuable experience, not only for learning to know each other but for discovering new things about ourselves. My dad thought it was a good thing too. Guys who had known him for twenty years said they had never seen him so happy. Besides he grew a beard along the way and he even kept it because he likes it."

Whatever could have prompted such an unusual graduation gift? Big Ed says:

"I didn't want to let my son slip into the demands of a career before we discovered each other. I was sure he was my kid, but I found out he's not just my kid, he's good people."

Isn't that a super thing to discover before a boy leaves home?

Most dads couldn't afford two motorcycles, or even one. Some of us shouldn't be on a thing like that even if we could afford it. But the story of those two Eds sure makes me think—what *could* I be doing to discover my children as good people?

CHAPTER 48

How Johnny Won First Prize
with His Hooked Rug

Johnny won first prize at the handcraft fair. There are many of these fairs in New England and the competition is terrific. You have to be good to win first prize. But for the grand first prize you have to be superior and Johnny is superior.

Nothing so unusual about that maybe. Except in this case—the prize winner was a magnificent hooked rug. Designed by Johnny, worked by Johnny, shown by Johnny; and Johnny is a high school junior.

Johnny doesn't care about sports. They're not his thing. He doesn't care about math, English, history, science, any kind of school work. Nothing in the study line, no teacher, no book has ever turned him on. Some way he's managed to pass, but the entire scholastic syndrome has been a drag for Johnny and for his folks. To which an echo all over the land, "Join the club. Same for my Johnny. My Susie."

So what do you do with a child like this? If you're Johnny's mom or dad, you keep your eyes open. You watch. Any spark of interest anywhere?

It was his father who picked up the first clue. They had gone to a handcraft fair when Johnny was in the seventh grade. They saw a potter at his wheel, a maker of brooms, a tall skinny man carving and bending his wooden pitchforks. Then they came to the rug hookers. Something clicked in Johnny. He liked that. One at a time, little bits of yarn, beautiful colors, thick nap, warm blending.

Fascinating. So on impulse they bought a little rug with all the makings. They took it home. Night after night they took turns hooking. And when it was done, Johnny wanted to know could they get another. And another.

Then he began to wonder, "Why don't I make my own designs, choose my own colors? Bet I could make some neat ones."

Good bet, Johnny, nice going, we're proud of you, you're a champion. But so is your dad. And so is every dad who keeps bird-dogging for any little interest which can be turned into a winner.

CHAPTER 49

Have You Hugged
Your Kid Today?

"Have you hugged your kid today?" It's a bumper sticker seen often in certain areas. And if you drove around Miami, Florida, you couldn't have missed it. Reason? The Dade County Mental Health Association promotes family seminars based on this unusual theme, "Have you hugged your kid today?"

Three doctors on the program tell why they believe physical closeness makes a big difference.

Doctor 1: "A child who does not get enough hugging or cuddling may grow up to be withdrawn, detached, aloof. Studies prove that body contact between parent and child is essential in child-rearing. It is so essential that in some cases children who are not hugged or cuddled during the first year of their lives do not survive."

Doctor 2: "Babies reared in an institutional situation are often found to be retarded in their social behavior. Frequently they will become 'passive and withdrawn.'

They may also have an extremely high mortality rate."

Doctor 3: "Whether a person is a hugger depends a lot on his upbringing. Usually if a child has been shown love and affection, he will give it in return. yet it is unfortunate that so many Americans do not feel free to express themselves physically. Too many have grown up with a form of love which limits itself to verbal expression, or none at all."

What difference does this "de-personalized" family background make?

To get some straight answers, I began studying certain of the de-personalized teenagers I know. And asking questions.

Some of them are so hung up they can hardly answer any question from an adult. They mumble, they go into a nervous laugh, act embarrassed, seem devoid of spontaneity.

But praises be, I also know other teenagers who aren't like that. These are the gracious, the open, friendly, warm.

What makes the difference?

Lots of answers, shading off into some things hard to understand. Yet always this one answer comes through loud and clear: The better blenders usually come from homes where love is freely expressed.

So it *is* a good question for any dad:

HAVE YOU HUGGED YOUR KID TODAY?

HAVE I?

CHAPTER 50

He Taught His Daughter to Smile

"My father deserves the Pulitzer Prize. There may be other fathers as good, but I don't think so. I could tell you many things about my dad, but here is just one thing he did.

"When I was a very little girl, my father took me into the bathroom and we stood in front of the mirror. Then he said, 'Sheila, you can see I am not very handsome. (That is true. He really isn't.) But you will see when I smile, I look a whole lot better.' And that is also true, because when my father smiles, he is beautiful. So he would say, 'Fortunately you don't look like me, but you are cute like your mother.'

"Don't you think that is neat for a dad to spend time with his daughter, actually showing her the difference?

"We would also sit in the car and watch people on the street. Whenever we saw someone who smiled, he would say, 'Can you see how much better they look? That is

111

someone you would like to know, isn't it?'

"But do you know how I learned the most about smiling and what it can do? I learned from the way dad smiles at me. He does this to encourage me. He does it after he scolds me. He does it any time like for instance, this morning. I ran into the bedroom with four curlers left in my hair and a toothbrush in my mouth. I said, 'Dad I missed the bus. Could you take me?' Now some dads wouldn't be like my dad. Some would let you know they didn't like it. But my dad opened his eyes and yawned. Then he smiled and said, 'Sure, you get ready and we'll go.' I think it is great to have a dad like that because he will smile at you when other fathers do not smile. And he also will take time to teach some things other fathers do not teach you."

CHAPTER 51

Appreciation for Good Music

One of the shortest musical criticisms on record appeared in a Midwest morning paper. It said simply, "A stringed instrument group played Wagner here last night. Wagner lost."

It must have been awful, but that's the way it goes. Some music is awful.

We were in a lively discussion one evening, a few dads talking it over, and some complaining about their children's music. "Too loud." "No melody." "Can't understand the words." Finally, when he'd had all he could take, a music teacher from the junior college stopped us cold with this, "Oh, come on you guys! Can't you remember 'Mares Eat Oats and Does Eat Oats and Little Lambs Eat Ivy?' How bright do you think that sounded to our parents?"

Then he tacked on this whammy, "*Any of you dads take any time at all for training your children to appreciate good music?*"

He made his point, and it is a good question. Whether we like our children's music or not, what have we done to educated them in symphony, opera, the classics?

Many of the young today are beginning to dig the oldies. They're open at least to hearing beautiful things from other countries, masterpieces from the past. Fitting right into this theme here's one paragraph from a recent letter:

"Most parents don't know there are records for introducing children to great music, even for very small children. Now and then, like every week or so, we have a family session when we listen to the classics. We read stories about them, and then we discuss. Can you imagine what music will be like when our little girls reach their teens? We can't. But we like to know they can at least come back to the lasting thing if they want to."

One more time, the man's question:

"Any of you dads take anytime at all for training your children to appreciate good music?"

CHAPTER 52

Hymn of Praise by a Daughter, Thirteen

Beth lives in New Orleans. She's thirteen and there probably isn't one father reading who wouldn't be grateful if his daughter felt like this:

"Dear Dr. Shedd:

"My father is one of the most considerate persons I know. We have nine children in our family, and he can always take a little time for each of us.

"But what makes him so unique is the way he treats my mom. At dinner he pulls out her chair for her. He never fails to tell her how good the food is, and he always kisses her first when he comes in the door. We try to trick him into kissing one of us first, but he always laughs and kisses mom first. Then he kisses us.

"Another thing which we all love is our mealtimes. For example, when I go to a friend's house, it takes them about ten minutes to eat and nobody talks hardly at all or if they do, they don't say anything important.

"At our house it takes us 45 minutes to eat and we can talk, really talk to each other. We decided a lot of important stuff and everybody gets to tell what they think. If there is something you don't like, you can say so and have it discussed. Not many of my friends can do that with their parents.

"My dad never hesitates to say 'please' when he asks us to do something, and 'thank you' when we do it. Here's another thing he does which not many dads do. He always says he's sorry when he is in the wrong. Of course, I suppose I should add we know he is not perfect, but all of us think he's the greatest."

Loving the mother well, living under the code of plain old-fashioned manners, listening, letting each person share his thoughts, all this takes time.

Thanks for writing, Beth. It's a beautiful tribute to a beautiful dad. I think any reader who ponders your words can see why you (plus your eight brothers and sisters, and your mother) say,

"All of us think our dad is the greatest."

CHAPTER 53

Settle It with a Slow Walk

"Dear Dr. Shedd:

"I first have to tell you that today is a most wonderful day. It's sunny outside, a little windy, but beautiful. The sun is bright, and the plants are clean and green, the sky is blue and most of all it's quiet. What a wonderful opportunity to write about my dad.

"Never have I written to a newspaper or for that matter for anything outside of family letters, but this is an opportunity I will not pass. Even though my writing is amateur, the love for my father could make me do almost anything. English is my second language. I was raised to speak Austrian.

"My father believed that you could really have togetherness if you would take the time for a slow walk with each other. When you had a problem, you could settle it by walking and discussing it. If you were angry, the thing to do was to walk it off while you talked about it.

"During the years when a child has so many questions and a young person is shaping his philosophy, a parent and child walking together could be just the thing.

"Sometimes we would walk on the railroad tracks and sing. We would pretend all kinds of things. Somehow everything would take a special color when we were together. I felt nothing could happen to me as long as my father was by my side. His hand became a grip on life.

"There is no way I can tell you all the things we settled together on a slow walk.

"My father is half blind now, but he still manages some special walks with his grandchildren. I'm glad my children have a grandfather like that, because I know they learn from him like I did.

"I wonder if a lot of families wouldn't do better if the father took some time for a few slow walks with each one of his children."

CHAPTER 54

Harold Is a Podiatrist

Harold is a podiatrist, which in layman's terminology, is a foot doctor. Or as Harold puts it with a grin (I can never tell when he's kidding), "I am a tender of the pedal extremities."

Now why would anyone choose to be a foot doctor? Harold says his father was partially responsible and here's the report:

"My father was a core maker, and when I was still in grade school, he dropped a casting on his foot, crushed it badly, broke so many bones he was laid up for weeks.

"He and I were very close, so it was natural I should ask questions: How was he feeling, when would it get better, how soon could he walk again? Then he would tell me all about it, and one day he offered to take me with him to the doctor.

"That was like my father. He never missed one single opportunity to follow up any interest of mine, including his sore foot.

"Well, the doctor was a very kind man who let me ask questions, gave me some pamphlets and a booklet or two. My father and I read these together and somehow we got the message that the human foot is an amazing mechanism. Several more times he took me back to the doctor, and I always remember this one thing the doctor said: 'Son, have you ever stopped to realize that when people hurt in the feet, they hurt all over? I know that's true, because when I do something to improve their feet, they improve all over.'

"Well, I thought about that and to make a long story short, I finally decided on a career in medicine. Then when it came time to specialize, I remembered the doctor's words again, and here I am, a podiatrist!"

So why this tale of "pedal extremities"? Maybe one good answer is Harold's statement:

"My father never missed one single opportunity to follow up any interest of mine, including his sore foot."

CHAPTER 55

Friday is Warm Fuzzy Day

Anyone around here need a good word?

Fred teaches school in Des Moines. Fifth grade. He's been teaching long enough to know basic needs and he says: "I've never had one child go through my classroom who didn't need affirmation. I also never had one who got too much of it if it was the right kind.

"So because I believe that, I worked out a ritual which we call 'Warm Fuzzy Day.' This is a term I first heard from one of our school psychologists and it stands for praise and compliments or anything which says, 'You're special!'

"Here is how we do it. On Monday I announce, 'this is Robert's warm fuzzy week' or Susan's or whoever is chosen. During the week each member of the class is expected to do one nice thing for that student.

"Then on Friday the chosen one comes to the front of the room and each member of the class tells him, 'I like you because . . .'

121

"Of course, I make sure that every child has his day, or hers every year.

"There is no way I can tell you what an improvement this has brought to our classroom, or what a difference it has made in my teaching. Also I want you to know real miracles have taken place in the lives of some of these students. Too many of them never get any commendation at home, not even one word of praise. But even with those children, the giving and receiving of affection has an amazing effect. All of us seem to become happier, more outgoing, and much more thoughtful. I have even had parents tell me, 'This year my child is a different child at home.'

"Do you know what I think? I believe everyone on earth would become a better person with just one 'warm fuzzy day.' "

Thanks, Fred, for telling us how you do it. Could be just the thing for some fatherly adaptations right here at home.

CHAPTER 56

They Burn Their Wrongs

"They burn their wrongs and watch them go up in smoke."

"Dear Dr. Shedd:

"In one of your recent columns you wrote about the father who taught his children 'When you close the door to your bedroom at night, remember we are going to forget everything you've done wrong. Tomorrow will be a new day.' Well, here's another story something like that.

"Part of my boyhood was spent in Ecuador. My father was stationed there, so I had a chance to see some things not many other people see. I remember this one tribe who had a ritual which they performed every year. In it the members would put sticks in a pile. Each stick symbolized some wrong or something they would like to forget. Then their chief would light the fire and they chanted as they watched it burn.

"I was only a small boy, but it made a deep impression on me.

"Now here is the part which I thought might help someone. In our family every year before the end of December we have a similar ritual which we borrowed from the natives. Only we write out what we are thinking about and it's all in private unless we want to discuss it. We include anything we're sorry for, plus our resentments, grudges, and bad memories. Then we light the fire and get quiet while it burns. I can tell you it is a very meaningful thing to all of us."

I am sure there are fathers who will say, "That's a bit too much for our family."

But whether it be closing the bedroom door, burning sticks, burning papers, or by any other method, it's a wise father who can create a family spirit of genuine forgiveness for all.

CHAPTER 57

What Do You Do with Your Christmas Cards?

Roy is an unusual father. He and Marjorie have four children, from eleven down.

What can we do to keep our gang thinking big? Looking beyond themselves? Reaching out?

Here's one possibility straight from Roy. Every year before Christmas Marjorie decorates a basket for their Christmas cards. Every day when the mail comes, they read their cards and drop them in the basket. It's a big basket, because they have many friends.

Then beginning January 1, each night at dinner they take out one card. They read the names, the notes, the mimeographed letters, and think about these folks. Next day, Marjorie writes a note.

But that isn't all they do. Because they are a very religious family, they pray for their friends of the day. And in her note, Marjorie tells them, "Our family prayed for you last night."

Roy says, "We've been doing this three years now and it's amazing how many times we get a letter back telling us that on the day we prayed for that particular family, they had a special need. Do you know what we think? We think this is the best thing we do at our house to develop unselfish attitudes in our children. Marjorie and I also think it's a great thing for the two of us because we tend to get self-centered too."

I recently heard a child psychiatrist lecturing on "How to Keep Children from Going into the Silence." She said one reason they do this is that they concentrate almost 100 percent on themselves during their teens.

Since Roy's children haven't reached that age, there's no way of predicting for sure how they will react. But my guess it that all those years of early training will pay off.

Thinking of others, praying for others, always produces the kind of people we like to know. It also produces the kind of people most of us would really like to be.

And what would we like to be really? Nearly every dad I know would like to be the kind who can say to his family and mean it:

> "You are first with me
> And I want you to help me remember it.
> But I think we should remember too
> The wisest man who ever lived, said,
> 'Everyone on the face of the earth is
>   really a part of our family.' "